border to border • teen to teen • border to border • teen to teen • border to borde

TEENS IN THE U.S.A.

Teens in the U.S.A.

by Kitty Shea

Content Adviser: Sasha Vliet, Ph.D. candidate,
Department of American Studies,
University of Texas at Austin

Reading Adviser: Alexa L. Sandmann, Ed.D.,
Professor of Literacy,
Kent State University

Compass Point Books ✦ Minneapolis, Minnesota

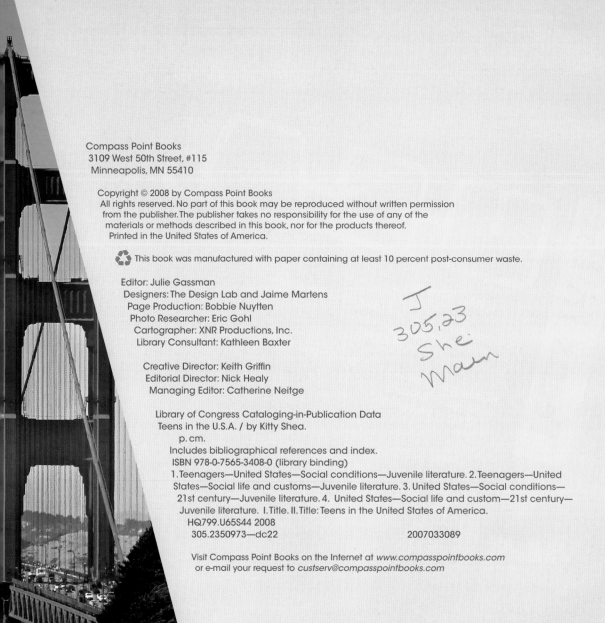

Compass Point Books
3109 West 50th Street, #115
Minneapolis, MN 55410

This book was manufactured with paper containing at least 10 percent post-consumer waste.

Editor: Julie Gassman
Designers: The Design Lab and Jaime Martens
Page Production: Bobbie Nuytten
Photo Researcher: Eric Gohl
Cartographer: XNR Productions, Inc.
Library Consultant: Kathleen Baxter

Creative Director: Keith Griffin
Editorial Director: Nick Healy
Managing Editor: Catherine Neitge

Library of Congress Cataloging-in-Publication Data
Teens in the U.S.A. / by Kitty Shea.
    p. cm.
Includes bibliographical references and index.
ISBN 978-0-7565-3408-0 (library binding)
1. Teenagers—United States—Social conditions—Juvenile literature. 2. Teenagers—United
States—Social life and customs—Juvenile literature. 3. United States—Social conditions—
21st century—Juvenile literature. 4. United States—Social life and custom—21st century—
Juvenile literature. I. Title. II. Title: Teens in the United States of America.
HQ799.U65S44 2008
    305.2350973—dc22   2007033089

Visit Compass Point Books on the Internet at www.compasspointbooks.com
or e-mail your request to custserv@compasspointbooks.com

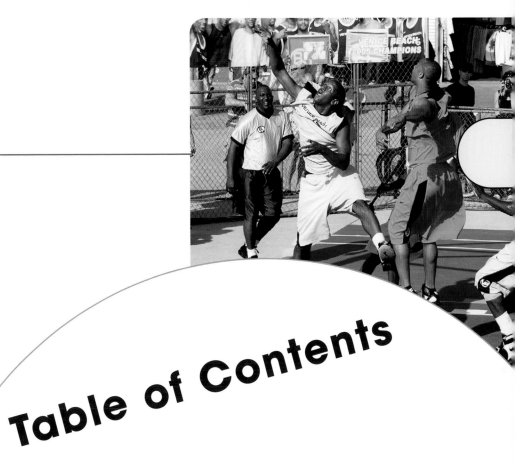

Table of Contents

PACIFIC
OCEAN

PACIFIC
OCEAN

CANADA

UNITED STATES OF AMERICA

MEXICO

CUBA

JAMA

BELIZE

GUATEMALA   HONDURAS

EL SALVADOR   NICARAGUA

PANAMA

COSTA RICA

ECUA

ICELAND

SCOTLAND
UNITED
KINGDOM
NORTHERN
IRELAND
IRELAND
ENGLAND
WALES

NETH.
BELGIUM

ITALY

FRANCE

TUNISIA

LIBYA

SPAIN

PORTUGAL

ALGERIA

MOROCCO

MALI

Washington D.C. ⭑

GUINEA

**ATLANTIC
OCEAN**

OM. REP.

FRENCH GU

GUYANA   SURINAME

VENEZUELA

MBIA

BRA

BOLIVIA

PARAGUAY

WHAT ONE WORD DESCRIBES AMERICAN TEENS? Ask a typical 14-year-old and you'll get a range of answers: happy, confused, hopeful, rebellious. The variety in responses is just one way to show the variety of teens growing up in the United States of America. There are, of course, some similarities. Most American teens attend school. Many are computer savvy and enjoy sports, movies, and hanging out with friends. But beneath these general similarities, there is wide diversity. Some teens grow up in high-rise apartments in crowded inner cities. Others live in spacious suburban homes with lush green lawns. Still others live on farms in what's known as the nation's heartland. And home environments are just the start in a long list of things that vary from teen to teen. Young people ages 10 to 19 make up 14 percent of the U.S. population. More so than older generations, these young people accept the differences that exist between one another. They love their friends—including the ones they've met only online. They believe the things that bring them together are more important than the things that divide them.

9

Students are often asked to complete assignments in small groups. Teachers use this method to give students experience working with a team.

CHAPTER ONE

The Basics & Beyond

FOR MANY AMERICAN TEENS, THEIR TIME IN SCHOOL IS NOT JUST FOR LEARNING. It is for social- izing and participating in activities, too. To see how this is true all it takes is a walk down a school hallway. Hanging on the walls are colorful posters announcing tonight's game, tomorrow's yearbook committee meeting, or next week's dance. Between classes the halls are filled with laughter. It's time to catch up with a friend, make plans for the weekend, maybe even flirt with that special someone. There isn't much time to spare,

however. Before long, the bell will ring, and it is time to get to class.

Teens enjoy playing for their school teams or singing with their school choirs. They like working with their class- mates on special projects such as planning the annual prom. But all the extras aren't just for fun. College admission officers are looking for more than good grades in prospective students. If students participate in activities, it shows that they are well-rounded and respon- sible. Extracurricular activities are one way for teens to stand out from the crowd.

How Busy Is Too Busy?

College admission isn't the only reason middle schools and high schools try to offer a variety of extracurricular activities to students. Studies have shown that kids who are involved with their school have higher self-esteem and are less likely to get into trouble. Teens say they like activities because they can try new things. They learn how to work in a team and get to know people they wouldn't normally hang out with.

In addition, some clubs provide an opportunity to learn things that are related to a career interest. A future reporter can gain experience with the school paper. A future politician can practice debate skills.

Staying Busy

Lack of funding can sometimes limit the options, but most schools offer at least a handful of choices for extracurricular activities. Here are some of the activities and sports available at U.S. schools:

Activities	Sports
Academic competitions	Baseball
Debate	Cheerleading
Diversity club	Cross-country running
Drama	Football
Math club	Golf
Newspaper	Soccer
Peer tutoring	Softball
Political clubs	Swimming
Science club	Tennis
Speech	Track and field
Student council	Volleyball
Yearbook	Wrestling

Staying Social

American schools provide students with opportunities to spend time with their friends outside of the classroom. The two social highlights of the year come in fall and spring with homecoming and prom.

Nearly every high school and college in the country holds a homecoming. Many schools celebrate homecoming for a whole week. Students are invited to dress up in costume to show their school spirit. The student body elects a king and queen, usually from the 12th grade class. In some schools, classes compete to see who can build the most impressive float for a parade held on Friday, homecoming day. After a football game on Friday night, there is often a dance.

In the spring, prom, a formal dance, often marks the near-end of the school year. The first proms were held in the 1920s. The boys wore jackets, and the girls wore their best dresses. The music was provided by a local band or a record player. In the 1960s, proms started to become more expensive. Boys started renting tuxedos, and girls bought expensive formal gowns that were worn only one night.

Today high schools often rent a reception area at a hotel. Other schools transform their gymnasiums into a dance hall with strings of lights, balloons, and streamers. Student-led prom committees are in charge of the decorating and all the details that go into the event.

Some couples spend an average of $800 to $1,000 on prom-related expenses, including renting a limousine and professional hairstyling.

Extracurricular activities foster a sense of school spirit. Teens come out to support their fellow students.

When students choose to participate in an activity, they have to be committed. Most activities take place during after-school hours, so teens give up some of their free time to join. Many activities require funding from the participants. They may pay a fee or be expected to help with fundraising. Selling candy, washing cars, or holding charity dinners are just a few ways that these school activities are commonly paid for.

Teens must find a way to balance their activity-filled schedules. If they take on too much, they can suffer from stress. They may become irritable and too tired to do well at their schoolwork. In 2006, the American Academy of Pediatrics (AAP) released a study showing that most teens are handling the pressures just fine. However, the report also warned that more and more teens are being diagnosed with anxiety and depression. To reach out to stressed-out teens, the AAP hosts a Web site to educate teens on stress and offer ways to reduce it.

School Is in Session

Of course, school in the United States isn't all extras; course work plays an important part, too. The school year generally runs from September through May, give or take a few weeks on either end. Students get most of June, July, and August off for summer vacation. Scattered schools operate on year-round calendars. These schools divide the long summer stretch into shorter, more frequent breaks throughout the year. Students may attend nine weeks of school, followed by three weeks of vacation, and so on, throughout the year.

On a typical school day, the bell generally rings between 7 and 8 A.M. The day is divided into a fixed number of periods, normally lasting around 40 to 50 minutes each. In some cases, classes may last from 75 to 150 minutes. This allows more time for covering material, helpful in science courses that require lab work. In most middle schools and high schools, students move from classroom to classroom, swinging by their lockers between classes to switch books.

Most school buildings are more than 40 years old. Despite their age, these facilities are generally well-lit, well-ventilated, and well-heated. Approximately nine out of 10 secondary schools have gyms, science labs, music rooms, and art rooms. Library media centers house books, magazines, and computers with Internet access. Teens—more girls than boys—use school libraries for assignments and casual reading.

Federal Rules in U.S. Schools

City and state authorities have the biggest say in running American schools. The federal government has long played a role, too. That role expanded in 2002 with the passage of the No Child Left Behind Act. The law seeks to improve school performance by tracking test outcomes. It requires students in grades three through eight to take standardized exams annually. If test scores repeatedly fall short at certain schools, the schools may be closed or their staff replaced. Private schools, however, don't receive government funding. Students there—who account for 10 percent of school-age children—don't have to take the No Child Left Behind tests.

In 2000, more than 98 percent of public high schools had vending machines. Since then some schools have banned them to limit students' access to unhealthy foods and drinks.

The average student-teacher ratio is 16 or 17 students per teacher. As a result, most classrooms are not too crowded. However, large class sizes can be a problem in lower-income school districts. (The larger the class, the more difficult it can be to learn.) Almost half of all urban high schools have 900 or more students. In contrast, half of all rural high schools have fewer than 300.

Where Kids Learn

The vast majority of teens—about 88 percent—attend public schools. These facilities are typically run by officials at the local and state levels. State officials determine school year length, curriculum themes, and graduation requirements. Meanwhile, locally elected town school boards deal with scheduling, equipment, staffing, attendance, and other day-to-day details. Local and state taxes (and, to a lesser degree, federal taxes) cover

Dressed for Success

While just 3 percent of public schools require uniforms, they are common in private schools. Boys' uniforms often feature polo shirts, sweatshirts, or sport coats with the school's logo. The tops are paired with navy, black, or khaki pants or shorts. With their polo shirts or blouses, girls may wear pants, jumpers, or skirts.

Even without uniforms, schools restrict what students wear. Dress codes spell out what is forbidden: clothing that reveals too much skin, is imprinted with offensive statements, or that advertises drugs, alcohol, or tobacco, for instance. To deter crime, some schools ban brand-name jackets, pricey shoes, fancy jewelry, and gang-related attire.

Those in favor of school uniforms claim that uniforms promote mutual respect, a focus on schoolwork, and school spirit. They say uniforms erase peer pressure to wear expensive labels. In an essay published by the magazine *Teen Ink*, one teen wrote about why she liked wearing a school uniform:

At my school, students came from diverse backgrounds. Inside the building, however, our economic advantages or disadvantages were no longer obvious. … This set the tone in the school system that all individuals were to be treated as equals.

However, many students complain that uniforms limit their right to self-expression. They believe, as one 14-year-old says, that wearing a uniform "doesn't allow you to express your uniqueness and individuality."

the average per-student cost of about $8,300 a year. Included in these costs are textbooks and other supplies generally provided by schools.

About 10 percent of U.S. teens go to private schools. These facilities are funded partly by tuition—fees paid by the students' parents. Financial grants and gifts made by private individuals and organizations also help keep private schools going. Most private schools are religion-based and supported by churches, mosques, or synagogues.

The remaining 2 percent of U.S. teens attend the most private of classes—those taught by their mothers and fathers around the kitchen table.

Homeschooling appeals to parents concerned about safety or negative influences at public schools. Parents may seek to provide their teenagers with religious or moral instruction as well.

Steve and Sandy Scoma of Columbia, South Carolina, home-schooled their four children. They felt they could give their children a better education than they could get at local public schools. Their son Sam said:

One of the things I like best about home schooling is you learn how to teach yourself. You can go to your parents for help, if you don't understand something, but you learn how to do research and find answers yourself.

In families that homeschool, parents are often teaching children of different ages at the same time.

While there's considerable freedom in choosing what's taught and how, homeschoolers must abide by state-set requirements. In Delaware, for example, they must register with the Department of Education. In Kentucky, they must keep attendance records. In Texas, they must include reading, spelling, grammar, math, and citizenship in their studies.

Courses & Graduation

U.S. teens in grades 9 through 12 take a fairly wide range of subjects. All take at least some basic math and science courses, which vary according to state requirements. All high school students must take basic English. In addition, most U.S. high schools require students to take at least one or

Typical Courses

Here's a sampling of the courses offered in American schools:

Math
algebra
applied math (budgeting and
    metric equivalents)
geometry

Science
biology
chemistry
geology
human anatomy
meteorology
paleontology

English
American literature
debate
effective writing
world literature

Social Studies
American history
current events
economics
geography
government
world history

Electives
art
business
consumer science
critical thinking
drama
foreign languages
health
music
physical education

two basic history classes, including American history.

Classes that are not required to graduate are called elective classes. These courses can vary throughout the country. In mountainous Colorado, students can take instruction in skiing. In many rural communities, courses in agriculture are offered.

Foreign language studies are among the more popular elective courses. The most common foreign languages offered at high schools are Latin, Spanish, and French. Some high schools offer Greek, German, Chinese, and other languages as well. Japanese has experienced the greatest enrollment leaps in U.S. high schools in recent years. Although foreign languages are usually not required to graduate, they are an admission requirement for some colleges.

In most schools, teachers specialize in certain areas, and students have a variety of instructors for their courses. Teachers use a number of teaching

Teachers use field trips to explain concepts. An anatomy teacher in Montana took some of his students to view human cadavers at an area university.

Computers play a major part in U.S. schools. Some schools offer laptop labs to make it easier for students to use computers in various courses.

methods. Some days students listen to lectures and jot down notes. Other days they may be asked to shove their desks together in groups of four. Team projects are an opportunity for students to work together and share ideas.

Whatever courses they take, and whether they attend public or private schools, nine out of 10 U.S. teens graduate from high school. Students need those degrees. A high school diploma is required for entry to college or vocational-technical school. It is also a minimum requirement for most entry-level jobs in the United States.

At the end of the school year, schools hold graduation ceremonies. Those who have completed their high school education walk down an aisle wearing a cap and gown. A stately song, *Pomp and Circumstance March No. 1*, likely plays. Often the student with the highest grades or one selected by the graduating class addresses the crowd of students, parents, and grandparents.

Then the happy grads collect their

The traditional hat worn by graduates is called a mortarboard.

reward: the diploma. In many schools, the graduates toss their hats in the air in celebration. That same day or soon after, parents host receptions for family and friends and display photos of their graduate's lives.

Of the students who drop out before graduating, boys slightly outnumber girls. African-American and Hispanic teens drop out at slightly higher rates than whites. In contrast, Asian-American teens are the least likely to drop out.

More than 60 percent of these high school dropouts eventually earn equivalent degrees after passing the General Educational Development (GED) Test. This exam covers reading, writing, math, science, and social studies.

Teen Scenes

A 14-year-old slaps her nightstand in search of her clock radio. Finding it, she silences an advertisement and tumbles out of bed. She has exactly 26 minutes to shower, choose an outfit, get ready, and grab a cereal bar before her ride honks from the road. Her parents are long gone, having left their suburban subdivision at dawn to beat the rush-hour traffic into the city, where they work. Luckily, several friends live nearby, and their moms carpool them everywhere. Two more years and she will have her own driver's license and the freedom to drive herself. She's counting the days.

Meanwhile, a 16-year-old in the city slings his messenger bag over his shoulder, inserts his iPod earphones, and starts his 12-block walk to his private arts high school. He would take the underground train, were it not for his mandatory stop at Starbucks for a tall freshly brewed latte. He really needs a java hit today to survive his first-period presentation on freedom of the press. He'd thought that going to an arts academy meant "all art, all the time."

But core subjects must be fulfilled in order to earn a diploma.

Far from the city, there's little traffic on the gravel road alongside which a brother and sister wait with their black Labrador retriever. They, like half of all students in the United States, ride buses to school. Their consolidated school serves three small towns. The girl's mind is on tonight's basketball game. The team has made the state tournament three years running, and this could be number four. Many of the local kids have farm chores to do. That's not the case with these siblings. Their parents used to farm full time, but they now hold service jobs in town and rent out their cropland. The yellow-orange bus appears, dust rising from its tires. Climbing aboard, the boy waves his baseball cap at the dog, urging the canine back up the driveway.

The backdrops of their lives differ, but school is at the center of their lives. They take the same courses and study many of the same topics as they prepare for their futures.

Teens use the Internet on a daily basis. They connect with friends, research personal interests, and use it to complete their homework.

2

Home & Its Many Comforts

TEENS IN THE UNITED STATES LIVE ALL OVER THE MAP, AND THEIR LIVES ARE ALL OVER THE BOARD. For most, home is the base of their comings and goings. Their rooms are sacred territory. They decorate them to their personal tastes, often to the displeasure of their parents.

But in general, most teens have to live by their parents' rules. Parents assign them household chores and curfews. Children are expected to eat meals with the family whenever possible. While at home, many teens keep a close eye on the outside world through the windows of their computer and TV screens. Many keep in nearly constant contact with their friends on their personal cell phones.

Even with all these comforts, you can't keep a teen home for long. Most enjoy more freedom than ever before. They are allowed to venture out into their neighborhoods on their own. (And for small-town kids, their neighborhood might be the entire city limits.) Young people have their opinions on the best places to work, shop, and hang out.

United States
Population density
and political map

N
W · E
S

0   150   300 mi.
0   150   300 km

Population Density
(People per square km)

More than 100   1–9
50–99   Fewer than 1
10–49

CANADA

Seattle
Olympia
WASHINGTON
Portland
Salem
OREGON
IDAHO
Boise

MONTANA
Helena

NORTH DAKOTA
Bismarck

MINNESOTA
St. Paul
Minneapolis   WISCONSIN

SOUTH DAKOTA
Pierre

Great Lakes

MICHIGAN

CANADA

MAINE
Augusta
Montpelier   N.H.
NEW   VT.   Concord
YORK   Boston
Albany   R.I.   MASS.
Hartford   Providence
CONN.
N.J.   New York

WYOMING

NEVADA
Carson City
Sacramento
San Francisco
San Jose
CALIFORNIA

UTAH
Salt Lake
City

Cheyenne

Denver
COLORADO

NEBRASKA
Lincoln   Omaha

IOWA
Des Moines

Madison   Lansing
Detroit
Chicago
INDIANA   OHIO
Springfield   Columbus
Indianapolis   W.VA.
ILLINOIS
Topeka   MISSOURI
Kansas City   St. Louis
Jefferson   Frankfort
City   KENTUCKY
KANSAS

PA.
Harrisburg   Philadelphia
Annapolis   Dover
DEL.
Washington, D.C.   MD.
Charleston   Richmond
VIRGINIA

Las Vegas

Los Angeles
San
Diego

ARIZONA
Phoenix

Santa
Fe

NEW MEXICO

OKLAHOMA
Oklahoma
City   Little Rock

ARKANSAS
Memphis

TENNESSEE
Nashville

Raleigh
NORTH CAROLINA
SOUTH
CAROLINA   Columbia
Atlanta
GEORGIA

PACIFIC
OCEAN

TEXAS
Austin
San
Antonio

Dallas

LOUISIANA
Baton Rouge
Houston   New Orleans

MISSISSIPPI
Jackson   Montgomery
ALABAMA

Tallahassee

ATLANTIC
OCEAN

MEXICO

Gulf of
Mexico

FLORIDA

Miami

ARCTIC OCEAN

RUSSIA

CANADA

ALASKA

Anchorage
Juneau

Bering
Sea

PACIFIC
OCEAN

HAWAI'I

Honolulu

PACIFIC
OCEAN

○ State capital
● Large city

Today only 25 percent of American families live in rural areas. A mere 1 percent live on actual farms. For the most part, the United States has become an urbanized society. About 45 percent of its residents live in the suburbs and 30 percent in city centers, the largest of which are New York City, Los Angeles, Chicago, Houston, and Philadelphia.

No matter where they live, American teens and their families come home to various kinds of dwellings. Single-family houses remain widespread, but people also live in condominiums, townhouses, mobile homes, and apartments. Of these families, about 70 percent own their homes.

The Urban Scene

Like cities around the world, American cities pulse with energy and variety. The country's urban centers are home to a huge array of shops and services. Residents live right next to, or often above, restaurants and stores. Downtown housing tends to take the form of multi-unit apartment, condominium, or loft buildings. Fanning out from there, blocks are lined with single-family houses on small lots. Families create their own communities within the cities. They visit their favorite delis and coffee shops, getting to know the people in the neighborhood.

Teens in large cities are likely to take public transportation to get

Jewish teens in Brooklyn, New York, celebrate the Jewish festival of Purim. Urban populations are more diverse than suburban and rural populations.

around. A common rite of passage for city kids is taking the underground train or city bus by themselves for the first time. In addition, urban sidewalks are filled with foot traffic. Having a car can be a hassle in major metro areas like New York, where parking can cost $575 a month or more.

Teen destinations in the city are many and varied. In addition to going to school and work, shopping, and running errands, young people seek out the large number of entertainment venues that cities provide. These include movies, plays, concerts, museums, and parties that feature music and dancing.

Urban areas have their share of problems. Poverty is more common in cities than in suburbs. Living in poverty can lead to other challenges. The housing conditions can give rise to unhappy, unsafe home settings in which people feel hopeless. This can lead some teens to take drugs, commit crimes, or join gangs. Community leaders strive to fund constructive activities for youth who have too much time on their hands. They believe that providing teens with focuses will keep young people out of trouble. These focuses include things such as structured opportunities to volunteer and teen centers where they can hang out. The majority of teens say they'd participate in these programs if they were available.

Home Sweet Suburban Home

America's population swelled in the years following World War II, and cities burst beyond their boundaries. The suburbs boomed! Today the suburbs continue to be a major American cultural realm. There, millions of teens are born, grow up, go to school, work, and later settle with families of their own.

These residential areas often

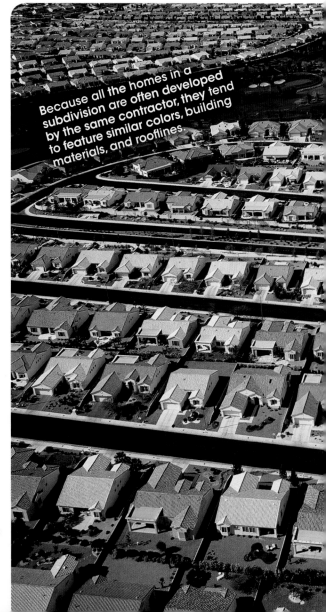

Because all the homes in a subdivision are often developed by the same contractor, they tend to feature similar colors, building materials, and rooflines.

feature subdivisions of single-family houses. Across the United States, home sizes are going up as family sizes go down. Today a typical suburban family has three or four family members (not including pets). They live in a home having more than 2,000 square feet (83 square meters).

Commercial areas are normally separate from residential neighborhoods. As a result, residents usually are required to drive to local businesses. However, modern suburban design is becoming more mixed-use. Many city planners prefer to feature one main street of businesses located in the center of neighborhoods. This design model is more pedestrian friendly.

Still, suburban teens spend considerable time in cars and minivans, such as the widely popular Toyota Camrys and Dodge Caravans. Parents shuttle

Drive Time = Talk Time

American families spend an average of 80 minutes in the car daily. The majority of parents use this time to chat with a captive-audience, their children. Topics range from school and extracurricular activities to friends and chores. Nearly 4 million miles (6.4 million kilometers) of public roads in the United States make for nearly endless opportunities for heart-to-hearts.

their offspring around until the kids can get their driver's licenses. (The legal age differs by state, with 16 being the average.) Forty percent of teens ages 16 and 17 have their own cars. By ages 18 and 19, that number jumps to 70 percent.

Country Living & Leaving

The lifestyles of teens in rural areas can seem a world away from those in cities and even suburbs. In general, crime rates are low. Rural parents feel they can send their kids outside to play with few worries. In fact, many residents think nothing of leaving

their houses unlocked and vehicle keys in the ignition. Small-town teens often know everyone in their entire school—along with their parents, siblings, relatives, and neighbors. Communities can't help but be tight-knit. Being close with your neighbors is a holdover from the days when farmers relied on their neighbors in order to survive.

These positive aspects of country life are frequently offset by some hard realities. One is the decline of the family farm. The number of family farms in the United States plummeted during the 20th century, mainly because of

Rural teens often drive around town to pass time, but high gas prices in recent years have kept some kids out of their cars.

United States
Land use map

N W E S

| | 0 150 300 mi. |
| 0 150 300 km |

Land Use
- Cropland
- Dairy products
- Forests
- Livestock
- Manufacturing
- Non-agricultural land

CANADA

Seattle
WASHINGTON

Great Lakes

CANADA   MAINE

MONTANA

NORTH
DAKOTA

MINNESOTA

MICHIGAN

NEW
YORK VT.
N.H.

OREGON

IDAHO

SOUTH
DAKOTA

WISCONSIN

Minneapolis

Albany

Boston
MASS.

Buffalo Syracuse

R.I.
CONN.

WYOMING

Detroit
Cleveland

Pittsburgh

New York

N.J.
PA.

Philadelphia

NEVADA

San Francisco
San Jose

UTAH

NEBRASKA

IOWA

Chicago
Toledo

INDIANA OHIO

Cincinnati

Baltimore
Washington, D.C.

DEL.

MD.

Denver

W.VA.

CALIFORNIA

COLORADO

ILLINOIS

KANSAS

Kansas City

St. Louis
MISSOURI

Louisville
KENTUCKY

VIRGINIA

Winston-Salem

Los Angeles

San Diego

ARIZONA

NEW MEXICO

OKLAHOMA

ARKANSAS

TENNESSEE

NORTH CAROLINA
Charlotte

Greenville SOUTH
CAROLINA

PACIFIC
OCEAN

Birmingham

Dallas

MISSISSIPPI

Atlanta

GEORGIA

ALABAMA

ATLANTIC
OCEAN

TEXAS

LOUISIANA

Houston

FLORIDA

ARCTIC OCEAN

RUSSIA

CANADA

ALASKA

Bering
Sea

PACIFIC
OCEAN

MEXICO

Gulf of
Mexico

HAWAI'I

PACIFIC
OCEAN

31

Teen Drinking

It is illegal for people under age 21 to consume alcohol in the United States. Yet 58 percent of 12th graders say they have been drunk at least once. Alcohol is teens' drug of choice. They are more likely to use alcohol than tobacco, marijuana, and other substances. Parents often underestimate how many, how early, and how much kids drink. By age 15, approximately half of America's boys and girls have had not just a sip, but a whole drink. Some have consumed considerably more. One in five people between ages 12 and 20 are binge drinkers, having downed five or more drinks in one sitting within the last 30 days.

Young people may not realize that drinking at any early age can affect them the rest of their lives. Studies have shown that kids who start drinking before age 15 are four times more likely to struggle with alcohol abuse than those who wait to be legal. Researchers also say teens who drink too much may suffer learning problems, including impaired memory.

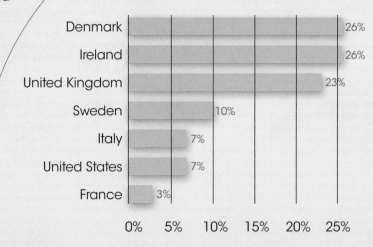

Drinking Habits of Teens
Percentage of 15- and 16-year-olds who were drunk 3 or more times in a 30-day period

Country	Percentage
Denmark	26%
Ireland	26%
United Kingdom	23%
Sweden	10%
Italy	7%
United States	7%
France	3%

0%   5%   10%   15%   20%   25%

Source: European School Survey Project on Alcohol and Drugs, 2003.

economic and technological changes. Today fewer than 2 percent of rural residents earn their primary living from farming. Instead, most rural Americans now work in service and manufacturing jobs. About two-thirds of rural people live close enough to metropolitan areas to commute to jobs located there.

Many young teens in small towns complain that they have nothing to do, especially at night. Bored, they smoke cigarettes and drink alcohol in greater numbers than their urban peers. Teen drug use, too, is often higher in rural settings than in cities. Poverty has a hand in these issues. Of the 250 poorest counties in the United States, 244 of them are rural.

Knock Before Entering

For many teens, their sense of place begins inside, in their bedrooms. Young people have been known to set up rules for their rooms. They control who's granted access, how the space is designed, and how clean and orderly it is.

In fact, one could argue that teens tend to treat their rooms like their first apartment. In some ways, this makes sense. The average teen's room functions as family room, study, lounge, game room, and sleeping quarters. Room makeover TV shows supply ideas for decorating. Catalogs and Web sites market the merchandise. Teens might shell out more than $350 decorating their rooms.

Bedroom decor often reflects hobbies and interests.

Shop & Spend

Where do teens get the cash to create their dream bedrooms? Some teens earn money by doing chores at home. Roughly nine out of 10 kids are expected to help out at home. Chore loads usually decrease when teens hit ages 16 to 18. Then they are busier with things like schoolwork, extracurricular activities, and jobs. Some teens get a weekly allowance, though the amount varies. A rule of thumb often applied by parents is $1 of allowance for each year of age.

These days, advertisers do everything they can to get teens to part with their money. About two-thirds of teens have savings accounts partly intended to protect the funds from temptation. About 10 percent of teens have credit cards on which they charge purchases.

According to a survey on materialism, teens ages 13 to 18 would rather spend time shopping than doing anything else. About 71 percent even say they'd be happier if they had more money to buy things for themselves.

Spying & Selling

Some companies hire teens to research other teens. These "cultural spies" carry cameras and tape recorders. They report back both the latest trends and the opinions and attitudes of their peers. Products are then developed to cater to the trend, but that doesn't mean the products will sell. As one cultural critic explains:

The minute a cool trend is discovered, repackaged, and sold to kids at the mall—it's no longer cool. So the kids turn to something else, and the whole process starts all over again.

The packaging and marketing of teen trends and culture pose questions about American culture. Which comes first: youth culture or a marketed version of youth culture? In other words, does the media simply reflect teen behavior and opinion, or are teen behavior and opinion formed by the media?

The message of materialism is fueled by advertising. Advertisers try to convince teens that in order to be considered cool, they need to buy what the advertisers are selling. Television commercials, magazine ads, and pre-movie spots in theaters have been shown to influence teens the most.

The commercial blitz also invades schools, where marketers' money helps compensate for cuts in government funding. The television show *Channel One* broadcasts news and public affairs content—plus commercials—to nearly 30 percent of U.S. teens during school. In addition, brand-name foods are offered in school cafeterias.

For all their purchasing zeal, however, many teens do spend their money unselfishly. Generally speaking, the majority of teens say they like to raise money for the needy, help new kids at school, assist others, and do favors for friends or family. In addition, most teens recognize they have a lot for which to be grateful.

Kitchen Duty

Teens are attracted to kitchens like magnets to refrigerator doors. For those who eat breakfast, the meal often consists of cereal with milk, toast with jelly, or bagels with cream cheese. Yogurt by the carton or squeezable

American grocery stores offer a vast array of products to shoppers. The average supermarket has 45,000 products.

tube offers food on the run. If there is enough time, families might enjoy a big breakfast with all the trimmings. This may include eggs; bacon, ham, or sausage; pancakes or waffles; and potatoes, beans, grits, biscuits, or rolls. Coffee or fruit juice, usually orange, washes it all down.

Noontime hunger is typically taken care of with soups, salads, and sandwiches. Lunch is often consumed at school or, for adults, at work. By the time teens get home from school in the afternoon, lunch is a distant memory. It is snack time! They devour candy bars, ice cream, potato chips, and cookies, and wash it down with soft drinks, juices, sports drinks, and iced teas.

Of the traditional three meals a day, the evening one—called supper or dinner, depending on the family—is usually the biggest. Meat and potatoes with a side vegetable is standard fare, but menus vary based on geography and cultural backgrounds.

American cuisine borrows from immigrants' traditions and regional specialties using local foodstuff. Southerners cover plates with fried chicken and grits, and New Englanders favor seafood. West Coasters toss together whatever's fresh and in season, since California is America's top agricultural producer. Texans ladle chili con carne into bowls, while Louisianans serve up gumbo. Different cities boast different signature foods: Chicago has deep-dish pizza,

I'll Have a Hamburger

From the time they savor their first McDonald's Happy Meal, many kids are hamburger happy. Those under age 18 eat more ground beef annually than any other age group. The world's most famous brand, McDonald's, began in 1948 in San Bernardino, California. Today the golden arches puts hamburgers into more hands than any other restaurant.

Away or at home, burgers get topped with ketchup, mustard, pickles or relish, raw or fried onions, American or other cheese, lettuce, tomato, mayonnaise, mushrooms, bacon, or avocado. The 2 percent of 8- to 17-year-olds who don't eat meat don't have to miss out on the fast-food experience. They can order veggie burgers and pile on the toppings.

Kitchens are typically used for more than meals. They may serve as playrooms, home offices, study spots, and hang out areas.

Omaha has steak, and Kansas City has barbecue.

Dinner may come from a bag, not the stove. Mealtime practices are moving away from formal rituals involving home-cooked meals. More and more take-out food is served.

Even with the ease of take-out meals, family members often struggle to be together for dinner. Only about 25 percent of 17-year-olds eat with their families nightly, partly because they are busy with school sports, jobs, and other after-school activities. Other reasons teens give for hiding around dinnertime include wanting to be alone, disliking the food being served, and being unhappy with their families.

American teens are often friends with those of the opposite sex. Dating is often done in groups.

3 Those Who Matter Most

AS AMERICAN CHILDREN GROW UP, THEY BECOME LESS DEPENDENT ON THEIR FAMILIES AND MORE DEPENDENT ON THEIR FRIENDS. About 58 percent of kids ages 8 to 12 prefer their parents' company to their friends'. However, that number quickly declines as they enter the teen years. Just 22 percent of teens ages 13 to 17 prefer to spend time with their parents, compared to 56 percent who prefer the company of their friends.

Most teens say they have between one and 10 friends. This number increases considerably when adding in friends they've met only online. Teens who use the Internet are connected to an average of 75 people via social networking sites like Facebook or MySpace. And they average more than 50 people on their Internet messaging (IM) buddy lists.

Studies show that teen girls are more likely than boys to have a wide circle of in-person friends, as well as a best friend. Female friendships are close. Girls love to have long conversations and share secrets. In contrast, boys tend to forge looser attachments and are less likely to confide in one another.

About 79 percent of U.S. teens are friends with someone of a different race, religion, or sexual orientation. This is a change from earlier generations, which categorized others by their differences. Increases in the numbers of women who work, immigrants joining communities both large and small, and the emergence of gay teens have led to greater acceptance.

All the Differences in the World

In the past 50 years, towns across the United States have combined members of ethnic groups from around the world. Most white teens trace their ancestry to Europe. The second largest group—Latin American teens—are mostly from Mexico and Central America. African-Americans—the third-largest ethnic group among teens—trace their lineage mostly to slaves

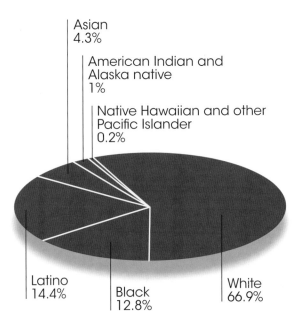

Ethnicities in the United States

Asian
4.3%

American Indian and
Alaska native
1%

Native Hawaiian and other
Pacific Islander
0.2%

Latino
14.4%

Black
12.8%

White
66.9%

Note: Because some people are more than one ethnicity, they may be included in more than one category.
Source: U.S. Census Bureau, 2005 estimate.

who were captured and brought to the Americas from the 1600s to 1800s. Other teens have roots in China, Japan, Korea, Vietnam, and other Asian countries. Native American teens are descendants of America's first inhabitants, who arrived at least 15,000 years ago.

Of nonwhite minorities, Latin Americans are the fastest-growing

Life on the Reservation

Less than 1 percent of the U.S. population is Native American. Currently one in three Native Americans lives on a reservation, land that the U.S. government set aside for them.

Indian tribes have sovereignty, which means they govern themselves. The operation of casinos has brought wealth to certain tribes. Unemployment rates on other reservations can exceed 65 percent. This leads to high poverty levels.

These sorts of conditions on the reservation make life especially challenging for many Indian teens. Native youth are at higher risk of substance abuse, suicide, and teen pregnancy than all other groups in the United States. Only 52 percent finish high school versus the national average of 90 percent. Of these, 17 percent continue on to college, but only 4 percent graduate.

group. This growth is partly from immigration, both legal and illegal, and from birth rates that outpace those of other ethnicities. Representing nearly 15 percent of the population, their numbers are making Latinos increasingly influential. For example, companies and businesses now market products and services to this population.

Still, the welcome mat is not always laid out. Like other minority

Latino Influences

One in five children under 18 in the United States is of Latin origin. In Los Angeles, it's four in five. By 2025, the Latin teen population is expected to increase by 50 percent, compared with only a 6 percent jump in the overall teen population. Latin influence on American culture cuts across many cultural spheres, including music (Christina Aguilera, Shakira, Carlos Santana, and Marc Anthony), movies (Penélope Cruz and Salma Hayek), television (George Lopez and Ugly Betty), fashion (JLO by Jennifer Lopez), and food (trendy Nuevo Latino).

Tagged "Bi-Bi" for "bicultural-bilingual," Latin American teens straddle two worlds. They hold fast to family bonds but feel the need to mainstream with American teen culture.

Often they function as cultural bridges for family members.

Seventeen-year-old José F. Ponce Granados came to the United States from Mexico when he was 12. He shared some of his experiences:

My English skills were very poor. The language was the first problem I faced, and I still have trouble speaking sometimes, but there are people who help me out. The second problem I faced was the culture and way of life. The cultures of Mexico and the United States are not too different, but still there are some things that are very different. The food, such as the lunch in school, was very different from what I used to eat in my country. With time, I started to get involved with my new lifestyle.

Latinos are the majority ethnic group in Los Angeles, California. East Los Angeles, the city's oldest Latino neighborhood, is 98 percent Latino.

groups, Latin Americans sometimes encounter discrimination in workplace hiring, firing, and promotions. The same kind of unfair treatment can arise when families go to rent or buy a house. Part of the reason for this may be too little political representation in government. The number of Latin Americans holding elected office is not yet balanced with their population.

God Bless America

As a rule, American families are not shy about their religious beliefs. For the majority of Americans, this includes a strong belief in God.

Numerous national institutions and customs acknowledge God's existence. For example, U.S. currency is emblazoned with the words "In God We Trust."

The image or name of God—especially for Christians—is also invoked in various American customs. Crosses, a symbol of Jesus Christ's death on the cross, are worn as pendants and earrings. Some teens wear wristbands inquiring "WWJD?" or "What Would Jesus Do?" These customs demonstrate Christianity's popularity in the United States. Surveys show that 88 percent of teens believe Jesus lived, 74 percent

Church Here, State There

One of the guiding principles of life in the United States is that God's work and the government's work should be separate. The first words of the First Amendment to the Constitution of the United States read, "Congress shall make no law respecting an establishment of religion, or prohibiting the free exercise thereof." That means the government cannot interfere in religious matters, including where citizens express their spiritual beliefs. But what about prayer in public schools?

This controversial issue directly affects teenagers and other young people. Teachers and public school officials are forbidden by law to lead their classes in prayer, devotional readings from the Bible, or other religious activities. In addition, they cannot encourage student participation in such activities. Students, however, are free to read Scriptures, say grace before lunch, or study religious materials, as long as they are not being disruptive.

believe Jesus is the Son of God, and 72 percent believe in Jesus' resurrection (celebrated on Easter Sunday).

Teens from non-Christian traditions are active in their faith in similar ways. Muslim Ambreen Ali, for example, is a member of a youth group, Muslims in Action. "We have a lot of different activities, including fundraisers for such things as tsunami relief and

Religion in the United States

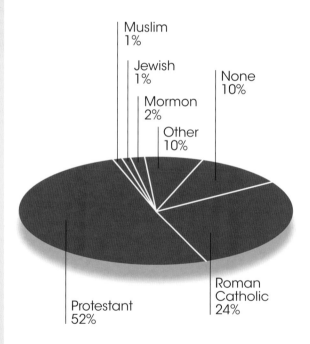

- Muslim 1%
- Jewish 1%
- Mormon 2%
- Other 10%
- None 10%
- Roman Catholic 24%
- Protestant 52%

Source: United States Central Intelligence Agency. *The World Factbook*—United States.

Christian rock concerts are extremely popular with teens who are active Christians.

humanitarian aid for people in Iraq and Afghanistan," she said. "We raise money in a lot of different ways, including bake sales and car washes."

In general, two out of three teens say that their religious views mirror those of their parents. Teens actively practice their faith through worship, prayer, and faith-based clubs and camps such as Young Life, National Conference of Synagogue Youth, and Muslim Youth of North America. More than half attend religious services at least monthly, and 40 percent pray at least once a day.

Family Portraits

There are many variations of the traditional family in the United States. Married couples still head about 63 percent of households. Twenty-six percent of households are headed by single women, and 8 percent by single men. In addition, about 8 percent of U.S. teens and other children live in a grandparent's home or have a grandparent living with them.

With just over 40 percent of marriages ending in divorce, the United States has the highest divorce rate in the world. Often, this means stepparents are in the picture, too.

The number of teens with siblings has been going down in recent decades. The average family size in 2005 was about three members, and only 6 percent of families have four or more children. Moreover, families with six or more kids are so rare that the U.S. Census Bureau no longer gives them their own category. The trend toward smaller families began early last century, when the country's agriculture-centered society became more industrial. Many parents no longer needed extra farmhands. In addition, access to better birth control, the entry

of large numbers of women into the workforce, and the rising cost of raising children further reduced family size.

Better methods of birth control, along with easier access to it, have also affected sexual customs among teens. In 1991, the pregnancy rate for girls ages 15 to 19 was 116 per 1,000. By 2000, the rate dropped to 85 per 1,000. It has since continued to decline. Experts attribute this drop partly to increased use of birth control, particularly condoms. Condom use among teens ages 15 to 17 increased by 30 percent between 1991 and 2000.

Other factors seem to have contributed to the decline in teen

What's in a Name?

Most popular names of the 2000s in the United States:

Girls' Names	Boys' Names
1. Emily	1. Jacob
2. Madison	2. Michael
3. Emma	3. Joshua
4. Hannah	4. Matthew
5. Abigail	5. Andrew
6. Olivia	6. Christopher
7. Ashley	7. Daniel
8. Samantha	8. Joseph
9. Alexis	9. Ethan
10. Sarah	10. Nicholas

Social programs help young mothers manage parenthood with education. The Care Center in Massachusetts provides mothers with an onsite daycare as they work toward their GED.

pregnancies as well. One is the expansion of sex education programs in many states. About 89 percent of students take at least one such course in either middle school or high school. The information taught is decided at the local level. Some sex-ed programs present facts about both contraception and the safer path of abstaining from sex. Other programs teach only the concept of abstinence. Nevertheless, the present teen pregnancy rate among 15- to 17-year-olds—44 for every 1,000 girls—remains the highest among the world's most developed countries.

Many teens buy gifts for their loved ones to mark holidays.

4

Days of Honor, Days of Rest

HOLIDAYS AND OTHER SPECIAL EVENTS ARE FAVORITE TIMES FOR AMERICAN TEENS. At the least, these days provide a break from school and other responsibilities. At the most, they are special occasions filled with family traditions.

The calendar provides plenty of opportunities for celebration. In fact, August is the only month that does not contain a major holiday in the United States. It does, however, feature the most birthdays, since more Americans happen to have been born in that month than in any other.

Americans spend a great deal of money buying presents and decorations to celebrate many of these occasions. They shell out an estimated $7 billion for Halloween, for example, including $2 billion for candy alone. And they spend a whopping $200 billion on Christmas decorations, cards, and presents. In fact, a large portion of the money that teens earn from their allowances and part-time jobs ends up paying for Christmas, Valentine's Day, and birthday presents for relatives and close friends.

Royalty for a Day

Birthdays are Americans' number-one reason to party. Parents often let teens come up with their own party themes—paintball, *High School Musical,* beading, spa, wakeboarding, *American Idol,* tie-dye, dance fever, or extreme sports. No matter the theme, pizza and cake are often on the menu.

Some birthdays are considered extra special. A girl's sweet 16 is a milestone. Trends show that wealthy parents are throwing their daughters over-the-top galas, featuring posh décor, four-star food, and expensive entertainment. More modest gatherings, however, are far more the norm.

Individual cultures have their own coming-of-age events. Those adhering to Spanish and Latin American traditions hold the *quinceañera* for 15-year-old daughters. American Jewish girls at age 12 have bat mitzvahs and boys at age 13 bar mitzvahs, denoting their crossovers from childhood to adulthood. For many Christian churches, the rite of confirmation symbolizes teens' conscious commitment to the faith. In each case, families balance the religious with the social. Following the ceremony, parents often host a party and invite friends and extended family to celebrate with them.

quinceañera
keen-see-AHN-nyair-ah

A typical quinceañera includes a dinner and a formal dance.

The First of Many Holidays

The first holiday of the year, New Year's Day (January 1), is usually a relaxed day since many Americans start the new year tired. They stay up late on December 31, following a New Year's Eve custom. For 100 years, crowds have gathered in New York City's Times Square to watch a ball drop down a pole as the clock strikes midnight and the new year rolls in. Today millions of people from all around the world watch the ball drop on television in their homes.

For many families, New Year's Day traditions involve little more than sitting in front of the television to watch football games or large-scale parades. In the South, it is a tradition to eat a meal of black-eyed peas and collard greens for good luck in the new year.

Valentine's Day falls on February 14. This holiday is especially popular among people in their teens and 20s. While younger children enjoy parties in school, teens typically exchange valentines and gifts with sweethearts and other close

National Holidays

Holiday	Day Observed
New Year's Day	January 1
Martin Luther King Jr. Day	Third Monday in January
Presidents' Day	Third Monday in February
Easter	Sunday in March or April (varies)
Memorial Day	Fourth Monday in May
Independence Day	July 4
Labor Day	First Monday in September
Columbus Day	Second Monday in October
Veterans Day	November 11
Thanksgiving	Fourth Thursday in November
Christmas	December 25

American Weddings

About 88 percent of Americans marry at least once in their lifetimes, which makes for a lot of weddings. Teens often serve as bridesmaids, personal attendants, groomsmen, or ushers. They dress in gowns and tuxedos and carry or wear flowers. Most weddings take place in churches or outdoor settings on Saturday afternoons, with festivities spilling into the evening. Guests sit solemnly during the ceremony as the couple exchanges vows. But when the official in charge introduces "Mr. and Mrs. X," those assembled break into applause. And then the couple strides down the aisle to grand music.

The mood is more relaxed at the reception, dinner, and dance afterward. Champagne (for the adults) flows freely, and toasts are made honoring the couple. Chicken, beef, and fish are typical main courses. Tiered wedding cakes are the time-honored dessert. The first dance belongs to the couple. Costs for such affairs are usually picked up by the bride's parents, the couple, or both. The price tag averages $27,500.

Couples often light a candle together as a symbol of unity.

friends. They also give cards, candy, flowers, stuffed animals, and other presents to family members. Valentine's Day is also the busiest day for getting married in Las Vegas, Nevada, where more weddings are performed annually than anywhere else in the United States.

Traditional Spring Celebrations

As the months roll by and spring arrives, many Americans celebrate Easter, the holiest day of the year for Christians. This day observes Christian belief in the resurrection of Jesus Christ. Churches fill with worshippers. Some teens take part in Easter-related services, including Passion plays, which tell the Easter story.

Easter also features several popular nonreligious customs that many young children participate in. Chief among these is the Easter egg hunt. The mythical, much-loved Easter bunny hides decorated eggs or plastic eggs filled with jelly beans and chocolates. The children then find and gather these treats. Meanwhile, their older brothers and sisters watch from the sidelines while enjoying Easter candy themselves.

Another spring holiday, Mother's Day, is celebrated on the second Sunday in May. Nearly 90 percent of Americans honor their mothers with cards, flowers, perfume, gift cards, books, and CDs. It is also customary in many families to honor grandmothers and godmothers, along with sisters and aunts who have had children. Fathers enjoy a similar holiday on the third Sunday in June.

A teen girl leads an Easter procession. Teens often take part in worship services as altar servers.

53

Celebrating America

The summer season moves into high gear after Memorial Day. Often marking the end of the school year, the holiday pays honor to U.S. veterans who have died in military service. American Legion members (veterans who served in the armed forces during war time) host memorial services to honor the fallen soldiers. It is also a time to honor family and friends who have died. And as a kickoff to summer, friends and family members often get together for cookouts and picnics.

Another patriotic holiday follows on July 4, Independence Day. Americans plant themselves in lawn chairs or on street curbs to watch parades. Many teens take part in the parades. Young local pageant queens

Every July 4, an outdoor concert on the U.S. Capitol's west front lawn is part of the celebration in the nation's capital, Washington, D.C.

wave from sports cars. High school bands march to patriotic songs. Volunteers support their organizations by walking the parade route and handing out candy. All the while, spectators wave the "Stars and Stripes," America's red, white, and blue flag.

Meanwhile, parks become crowded with picnickers, who look forward to good food and good

company. The traditional food includes hot dogs, hamburgers, potato salad, potato chips, baked beans, corn on the cob, watermelon, and lemonade. Then, as daylight gives way to dusk, all eyes turn skyward to watch fireworks displays. Americans explode an estimated 220 million pounds (100 million kilograms) of fireworks every Fourth of July.

The first Monday in September, Labor Day, marks the unofficial end to summer. Like the other big summer holidays, Labor Day is celebrated with family picnics and sometimes parades and fireworks.

Autumn Splendor

Various polls have revealed that teens' favorite holiday is Halloween. Celebrated on October 31, Halloween is second only to Christmas in general popularity. Every year on Halloween, ghosts, black cats, graveyards, and cobwebs haunt lawns through which costumed children stomp. Ringing doorbells, they demand "Trick or treat!" and receive candy from those who live there. A favorite Halloween custom for families is hollowing out pumpkins and carving scary faces into them.

A fall vegetable, pumpkins also figure in the next major holiday celebrated across the United States. Thanksgiving is observed on the fourth Thursday in November. On this well-loved and festive day, family and friends gather to give thanks for their

A traditional autumn activity is visiting a pumpkin patch. The pumpkins are used in decorating and cooking.

blessings and share turkey and dressing, mashed potatoes and gravy, sweet potatoes, green bean casserole, cranberry sauce, and pumpkin pie.

The traditional Thanksgiving meal dates to 1621, the year after English Pilgrims arrived in Massachusetts.

Having lost half their population the winter before, the colonists sought the Indians' help growing crops and surviving. The next fall's harvest was bountiful, and the Pilgrims' special dinner later came to be celebrated across the nation.

Many states are famous for key

holiday ingredients. Minnesota leads the nation in turkey production. Wisconsin and Massachusetts are big producers of cranberries, while North Carolina grows huge amounts of sweet potatoes. Illinois supplies millions of pumpkins, while mountains of potatoes come from Idaho and Washington.

Not So Silent Nights

Christmas shopping season roars out of the gate the day after Thanksgiving. "Black Friday" is the day many retailers make enough money to put them in the black, or make them profitable, for the first time all year. Stores open as early as midnight, offering bargains to early-bird shoppers. Many businesses other than retail stores are closed that Friday, giving many Americans what amounts to a four-day weekend.

When they talk about the "holi-days," most Americans lump together the Christian holiday Christmas, the Jewish holiday Hanukkah, and the African-American holiday Kwanzaa as well as New Year's Eve and New Year's Day. For teens, these holidays mean a blizzard of school programs, parties, shopping, present-wrapping, religious events, good deeds, and community attractions such as tree lightings.

Given that the majority of Americans are Christian, it's no surprise

A Thanksgiving Day Tradition

Over the past half century, a number of popular televised Thanksgiving traditions have arisen in the United States. One is the Macy's Thanksgiving Day Parade in New York City, which began in 1924 but was not shown on TV until 1948. Its signature balloons— enormous, helium-filled icons such as the cartoon character Sponge Bob Square Pants—float down skyscraper-lined streets, wowing 2.5 million spectators. At home, another 50 million watch on television. Another Thanksgiving TV tradition is the watching of National Football League (NFL) games. Families gather and cheer on their favorite teams.

that Christmas gets the most attention in stores and on television. Christmas spirit is obvious both inside and outside the home. Glimmering lights in a carousel of colors trim rooflines, cover bushes, and entwine railings. Ambitious homeowners erect lavish displays featuring Santas, sleighs, reindeer, cartoon characters, and Nativity scenes. Communities sponsor contests for the best-decorated homes.

All is colorful and aglow indoors,

Seven Days, Seven Principles

A nonreligious holiday, Kwanzaa seeks to reaffirm African-Americans' roots in African culture. From December 26 to January 1, observers focus on one value a day for each of seven days. Its origins trace to the first harvest celebrations of Africa. Indeed, Kwanzaa means "first fruits" in Swahili, the most widely spoken African language. Dr. Maulana Karenga, a professor of black studies, created Kwanzaa in 1966. He wanted people to learn more about their history. Kwanzaa's seven principles are:

Umoja—Unity
To stay together as a family, community, nation, and race

Kujichagulia—Self-Determination
To be who you want to be

Ujima—Collective Responsibility
To work together and help one another

Ujamaa—Cooperative Economics
To support the community's stores and other businesses

Nia—Purpose
To work together to build the community

Kuumba—Creativity
To use one's talents and always do one's best

Imani—Faith
To believe in yourself and others

Umoja
oo-MOH-jah

Kujichagulia
koo-jee-chah-goo-LEE-ah

Ujima
oo-JEE-mah

Ujamaa
oo-jah-MAH

Nia
Nee-ah

Kuumba
koo-OOM-bah

Imani
ee-MAH-nee

Some families exchange gifts on Christmas Eve, while others wait until Christmas day.

too, with lights circling real or artificial pine trees bedecked with ornaments, tinsel, or strung popcorn. Mothers tend to lead the decorating activities, with the aid of their teens and younger children. They also hang stockings from fireplace mantels, drape pine boughs, and make showy crafts.

Teens place the presents they have purchased and wrapped under the Christmas tree. An estimated 96 percent of 8- to 18-year-olds in the United States give Christmas presents, with the majority buying the gifts rather than making them. When it comes to their own wish list, nearly 90 percent would most like money. Other requested gifts include

tech-related items, such as CDs and computer gear, followed by clothing and gift cards.

Usually in December, but occasionally in late November, Jewish families gather during the eight nights of Hanukkah. Together, they light the menorah, a symbolic candleholder. And starting December 26, some African-Americans spend Kwanzaa revisiting the seven principles rooted in their African heritage. According to a survey on what the holidays mean to today's youth, spending time with family is American teens' favorite part of the holidays. This is true no matter which religious or non-religious tradition they follow.

Teens as young as 16 can work as clerks in retail stores.

5

Making a Life, Making a Living

HIGH SCHOOL GRADUA-TION RATES IN THE UNITED STATES HAVE BEEN AT LEAST 85 PERCENT SINCE 1976. Diplomas in hand, teens now have some major decisions to make regarding what they are going to do with their lives. Should they continue their education at the college level? If so, which school, and how will they pay for it? Should they attend vocational-technical school and learn a trade? How about going right into the workforce or the military? Will they be doomed if they choose one path over another? Will they ever again associate "summer" with "vacation"?

Awaiting teens' decisions is the richest economy in the world. The country is prepared to deliver opportunities to those who possess the right stuff. Often the best of these opportunities require that high school graduates pursue higher education.

For this and other reasons, two in three teens choose to go to college following high school graduation. An estimated 17.6 million teenage college students descend on the United States' 4,000-plus colleges and universities each autumn.

Teen Labor

Even before high school graduation, many teens have already held a job. More than half of 16- to 19-year-olds in the United States work at summer jobs. They earn money and an introduction to the working world. The overwhelming majority of teen jobs are in hotel and food service (nearly 2 million) and retail (almost 1.7 million). These industries hire large numbers of temporary, seasonal employees and have few entry requirements. Whether waiting tables, cashiering, or folding jeans, teens work an average of 29 hours a week during their summer "vacations."

Sixteen is the minimum age for employment without great restrictions in the United States. Legally, kids under age 14 can deliver newspapers, perform certain farming chores, act in theatrical productions for pay, and babysit. Those ages 14 and 15 can bag groceries, stock shelves, prepare fast food, run cash registers, wash dishes, make photocopies, and file paperwork.

There are restrictions on their workday, however. Work must take place between 7 A.M. and 7 P.M. during the school year and no later than 9 P.M. during the summer. Teens 16 and older can perform all kinds of full-time jobs, from clerking in department stores to landscaping to waiting tables.

Detasseling—removing the tassel from the top of the corn to halt self-pollination—is a common summer job for rural Midwestern teens.

College Bound

Although the terms *college* and *university* are often used interchangeably, technically they have different meanings. By definition, colleges offer undergraduate programs that usually take four years to complete and lead to bachelor's degrees in the arts or sciences. Community or junior colleges generally offer two-year undergraduate associate arts and science degrees. In contrast, universities maintain several colleges as part of their systems. They also have graduate schools that award master's degrees and doctorates (known as Ph.D.s). Universities also contain graduate professional schools in fields such as medicine, law, and dentistry.

One of these degrees is often a stepping-stone to the next. Students who are less sure of their academic abilities, or those undecided about their futures, may start at community or junior colleges. These cost less but usually cover the same initial ground as four-year institutions. Upon attaining associate degrees, students may transfer to a college or university. Four-year grads whose goals require

Degrees = Dollars

Earning power for year-round, full-time workers in the United States directly relates to how much education they attain.

Highest Education Attained	Average Annual Salary
No high school diploma	$22,326
High school diploma or GED	$31,209
Some college, no degree	$36,371
Bachelor's degree	$51,436
Master's degree	$64,540
Doctoral degree	$85,774

Bachelor's degrees usually require four or five years of study; master's degrees usually require an additional two years; and doctoral degrees require an additional three to six years.
Source: U.S. Census Bureau, 2006

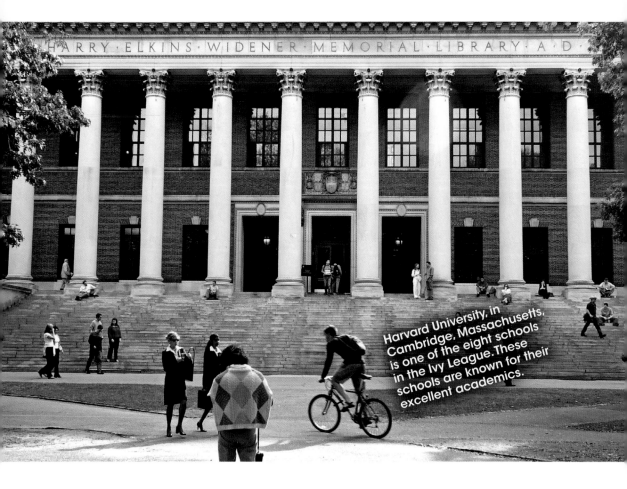

Harvard University, in Cambridge, Massachusetts, is one of the eight schools in the Ivy League. These schools are known for their excellent academics.

further study might pursue master's and then doctoral degrees. The education programs become more focused and specialized as students progress. Master's degrees typically require two years of full-time study, while Ph.D.s require three to six years.

Most students can choose between public and private colleges and universities. Costs vary significantly. Tuition and fees plus room and board for full-time students at public universities, where states help pay the bill, average more than $12,000 a year. At private colleges, which may be religious-affiliated or same-sex, the average tab is nearly $27,000. More than 60 percent of undergrads receive financial help from the federal and state governments, the school, or other sources. Many students depend on student loans, which average $5,800 annually and must be repaid after graduation. There are also work-study jobs to help students pay for school while they attend.

If Not College, Then ...

Those who aren't keen on college, or whose interests steer them toward a specialized field, may attend vocational-technical schools. There they learn the practical skills needed to be a computer programmer, automobile technician, carpenter, medical

assistant, or hairstylist, to name just a few. Vo-tech programs can take anywhere from several weeks to more than a year, and they result in certificates of completion or diplomas.

A number of other high school grads are drawn to the U.S. armed forces and the military's promise of education, travel, and job security in exchange for service. Active-duty

The Major Majors

The 10 most popular undergraduate majors, or programs of study, in the United States

1. Business
2. Social sciences (economics, political science, anthropology) and history
3. Education
4. Psychology
5. Visual and performing arts
6. Health professions and related clinical sciences
7. Communication, journalism, and related programs
8. Engineering
9. Biological and biomedical sciences
10. Computer and information sciences

Source: National Center for Education Statistics, 2006

soldiers, for instance, can get up to $72,900 to help pay for college through the GI Bill and the Army College Fund. Sailors in the Navy are allowed breaks from service in the form of 30 days of paid leave yearly. They also are allowed to hop on military flights for free. Hundreds of occupations in the military—health care, administration, electronics, telecommunications, and law enforcement, for example—can lead to jobs after military service ends.

Army and Marine Corps recruiting has been hurt by the U.S. invasion of Iraq in 2003. (Recruiting for the Air Force and Navy, two branches not heavily involved in the Middle East, has remained stable.) Parents fear their sons or daughters might be killed or injured. A recent U.S. Department of Defense survey showed that the percentage of parents who would recommend military service to their teenage (or older) children has fallen from 42 percent to 25 percent.

Gainfully Employed

Those teens who decide to go right to work after graduation tend to have varied perceptions about the

A Marine recruiter visits with a young woman. Military recruiters look for potential recruits in schools and public places such as malls.

working world. Often they've grown up watching both their parents work. Fifty-nine percent of U.S. women work outside the home, including three of every four mothers.

If current trends continue, teens can expect to work many hours. On paper, the American workweek is 35 to 40 hours. In practice, however, it is often longer. Many employers expect their workers to put in overtime. In fact, American workers put in more hours than those in any other industrialized country. One in three logs more than 40 hours per week, and one in five invests 50-plus hours a week.

Military Muscle

The armed forces of the United States protect U.S. interests around the world. A volunteer military, it consists of five branches and has more than 1.4 million active-duty and reserve members. Women are permitted to serve in most noncombat capacities and in a few combat assignments.

Army: The largest branch of the armed forces, the Army has 675,000 full-time active duty and reserve (part-time) soldiers responsible for land-based military operations.

Navy: Responsible for naval and marine forces, along with ships and submarines, the Navy carries out military missions at sea. It partners with the Marine Corps and, during wartime, the Coast Guard.

Marine Corps: A small, dynamic force, the Marines are considered the "soldiers of the sea," partnering as they do with the U.S. Navy on military expeditions.

Air Force: The youngest branch of the armed forces, it is responsible for military operations in the air and in space. Satellites and aircraft patrol for signs of hostile activity, while transport planes deliver troops and supplies.

Coast Guard: Stationed in maritime regions—along coasts, at ports, and on inland and international waters—the Coast Guard safeguards the country's public, environmental, economic, and security interests.

In addition, the average commuter spends about 50 minutes getting to and from work daily. Teens see the effects of these realities. Their parents have busy schedules, increased job-related stress, and decreased time with their children.

Experts say that there is likely to be favorable employment oportunities for members of Generation Y—Americans born from the early 1980s to the late 1990s. Jobs in hospitals, nursing homes, and residential care facilities will swell as the largest population subgroup in the United States—the so-called baby boomers—ages. Longer life expectancies are anticipated, compliments of better medicine. The field of education will also balloon. Student enrollments are increasing, from day care levels on up. These and other service jobs will account for a whopping 18.7 million of the 18.9 million new positions created by 2014. This trend shows that the United States is continuing its long-term shift toward a service economy.

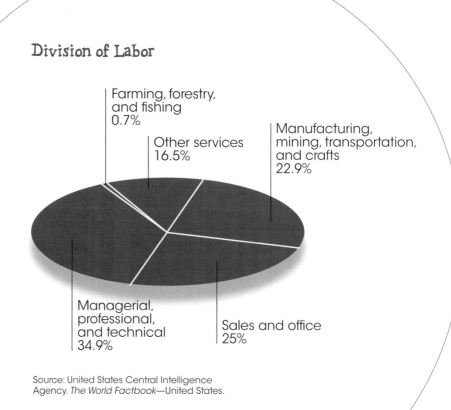

Division of Labor

Farming, forestry, and fishing
0.7%

Other services
16.5%

Manufacturing, mining, transportation, and crafts
22.9%

Managerial, professional, and technical
34.9%

Sales and office
25%

Source: United States Central Intelligence Agency. *The World Factbook*—United States.

A Good Cause

Millions of Americans balance time at work with time volunteering. Approximately 59 million Americans volunteer an average of one hour a week. Teens ages 16 to 19 are more likely to volunteer than any other age group under 35. Most teens work with religious, educational, or youth-related organizations.

Service learning is a requirement at many urban and suburban schools. As a result, more than one in four students under 18 are exposed to volunteering. What begins as a "have to" often blossoms into a "want to." Teens who at first dismissed the venture as "uncool" have been known to become impassioned about helping others.

Eighteen-year-old Kelsey Blom is a volunteer mentor to a fifth grader. She said:

Being able to impact another person's life is one of the reasons why so many teens are willing to give up their time to help others. ... Teenagers volunteer their time because they want to. They are doing it out of the goodness of their hearts, with no rewards in sight. But even though there are no concrete rewards, the skills and confidence that one gains are priceless.

As a service project, a teen boy helps build a new deck for a teen center in New Mexico.

Football was derived from the United Kingdom's rugby in the early 1800s. Many Americans love to both watch and play the sport.

6 Revved Up About Down Time

NO MATTER HOW MUCH TIME U.S. TEENS SPEND AT SCHOOL OR WORK, THEY ALWAYS FIND SOME FREE TIME. Popular pastimes are more numerous and varied than those available to teens in many other countries. This is because the United States is, overall, a wealthy country. Even many Americans whose earnings fall below the country's official poverty level have far more money, possessions, and social opportunities than poor people in other countries.

In addition to school-sponsored activities, young people pursue a large array of activities outside of school. Among the more popular are surfing the Internet, playing video games, reading books and magazines, and watching TV. Outside the home, teens like to go to movies and professional sporting events, attend religion-sponsored events, hang out at the local mall, and travel.

Saying Hello to Their First Cell Phone

Much of the average teen's free time is spent chatting with friends on the phone. Cell phones are status symbols that let teens text-message or gab with friends, play video games, and go online. All the while, they broadcast individuality via their chosen ring tones, screen savers, and faceplates. Carrying their first cell phone has become a rite of passage for U.S. teens. Three out of four 15- to 17-year-olds have a cell phone, despite being too young to purchase a calling plan contract themselves. (The magic age is 18.) Parents, thankful for a means of tracking their children's whereabouts, most often pick up the tab.

Sports, Music, Acting, & More

Of all these activities, playing sports remains one of the most popular among America's youth. And participation by teens has increased in recent years. According to the National Federation of State High School Associations, just over half of high-school-age teens take part in some form of athletics.

The biggest girls' sports are basketball, track and field, volleyball, fast-pitch softball, and soccer. Boys most often choose football, basketball, track and field, baseball, soccer, and wrestling. Both boys and girls also participate in tennis, golf, gymnastics, hockey and fencing, though in smaller numbers. In addition, there are so-called fringe sports—those outside the mainstream— that attract young people. These include skateboarding, snowboarding, surfing, canoeing, rock- or wall-climbing, judo, karate, kung-fu, and power-lifting.

Teen participation in creative and artistic activities is also quite high in the United States. Millions of young people join musical groups, including marching bands, school and church choirs, school and community orchestras, rock bands, rap groups, jazz ensembles, string quartets and other chamber music groups, barbershop quartets, and many more. Some of these young musicians and singers go on to play or sing professionally.

Another popular creative outlet is theater and drama. All across the United States, high school and college drama departments and community theater

In the early 1970s, just 7 percent of high school girls played sports. A federal law, passed in 1972, ensured that girls were given equal opportunities in education, increasing the amount of girls in sports. Today more than 40 percent participate.

groups perform plays. Professional regional theaters sometimes cast teenagers when the role calls for it.

A love for drama spills into film for some. Thousands of young Americans purchase or borrow cameras and experiment with making their own amateur movies. They are well aware that Steven Spielberg and numerous other famous and successful filmmakers started out doing the same thing.

Meanwhile, some teens pursue various areas of the visual arts, either as hobbies or as potential careers. These arts include painting, sculpture, digital art, and photography. Still other teens join clubs and other social groups, both inside and outside of school settings.

Home to Hip-Hop

The United States is the birthplace of several musical styles, including rock 'n' roll, blues, and jazz. Most recently, hip-hop has taken the country and world by storm. First developed in New York City in the early 1970s, hip-hop includes rap music, break dancing, graffiti, deejaying, and emceeing. It has become a whole cultural movement, influencing fashion, film, and television.

Today hip-hop has reached a global level. Countries such as Israel, France, Brazil, and Japan have their own hip-hop cultures. A writer for *National Geographic* commented:

Internationally, hip-hop has emerged as the world's favorite youth culture. Thanks to satellite TV and the Internet, kids from Valparaiso to Vladivastock rock [wear] Sean-Jean and Roc-A-Wear clothes, while the relative merits of Biggie versus Tupac are still a topic of intense debate in many languages.

Young hip-hop star Chris Brown's first CD was released in 2005, when he was just 16.

Hip-Hop Highlights

1979

The Sugar Hill gang releases *Rapper's Delight*, the first recorded rap record; Grandmaster Flash forms the Furious 5, one of the most influential rap groups of all time.

1980

Kurtis Blow records *The Breaks*, the first rap record to sell more than a million copies; the television network Black Entertainment Television, or BET, is founded.

1981

The Beastie Boys are formed; they release their first album, *License to Ill*, in 1986; the album goes platinum for the ninth time in 2001; in 1999, the Beastie Boys become the first band to win Grammy Awards in both rap and alternative categories with their single "Intergalactic."

1982

The first international hip-hop tour begins, exposing Europe and Asia to rap and hip-hop.

1984

The hip-hop label Def-Jam is founded.

1985

The first hip-hop martial arts film, *The Last Dragon*, is released.

1986

Run-DMC releases a hip-hop version of Aerosmith's "Walk This Way"; it is the first rap song to reach the top five on Billboard's Hot 100.

1987

Public Enemy releases their debut album *Yo! Bum Rush The Show*.

1994

Women rule the Grammy Awards as Queen Latifah becomes the first woman to win the Grammy for Best Rap Solo Performance for "U.N.I.T.Y." and Salt-N-Pepa is the first female group to win Best Rap Performance by a Duo or Group for "None of Your Business."

1996

Bone Thugs-N-Harmony break the record for fastest-rising single with "Tha Crossroads"; the title was previously held by The Beatles' song "Can't Buy Me Love"; Tupac Shakur is shot and killed in a drive-by shooting; a year later, the Notorious B.I.G., also known as Biggie Smalls, meets the same fate.

1997

Missy Misdemenor Elliott debuts with her first album, *Supa Dupa Fly*; Missy goes on to become the highest-selling female rapper of all time.

1998

White rapper Eminem breaks racial barriers when his debut album, *The Slim Shady*, races up the Billboard charts.

2006

Three 6 Mafia's "It's Hard Out Here for a Pimp" from the movie *Hustle & Flow* wins an Oscar for Best Original Song; this is the first time a rap song is performed at the Academy Awards.

Screen Time

When they are not participating in one of their many activities, teens often plant themselves in front of a television or computer screen. Nearly half of the homes in the United States have three or more color TVs. The average American youth spends 1,023 hours a year watching television—compared to 900 hours in school. As for the programs they watch, reality shows are wildly popular. Why? Experts suggest that it may be in part because teens can relate to the characters. Nearly one in three 13- to 18-year-olds feels that players on reality television are more like them than the people on regular TV. Even more believe that they could be contestants on reality shows. Sports coverage also attracts many teen viewers.

The often-cited charge that teens are glued to their TVs is technically inaccurate. Teens in the United States are media multitaskers who are able to watch TV and, at the *same* time, listen to music, read, and operate a computer! Similarly, one in four teens goes online

Video games also keep teen eyes glued to screens. The average playing session lasts more than an hour.

When Facebook first launched in 2004, only college students were allowed to join. A year later high schoolers were welcomed, and beginning in 2006, anyone could join.

to a TV show's Web site to play games, learn more about the show's characters or actors, or preview future or review past episodes—all while the current show is airing.

Another online draw for teens consists of social networking Web sites such as Facebook and MySpace. Facebook's 30 million active users post photos of themselves and their friends, write captions, watch videos, play tunes, display messages, blog, and chat with real and virtual buddies. It's very much their space in the sense that they feel it affords them the opportunity to express themselves.

More than 60 percent of them say they do things online that they would not want their parents to know about.

Shelving It

Even as millions of American teens roam the Internet, more become hooked on reading. The literacy rate in the United States is estimated to be 99 percent, one of the highest in the world. Studies indicate that three out of four 8- to 18-year-olds read for pleasure an average of 43 minutes a day. When it comes to books, girls' favorites include The Clique, A List,

Princess Diaries, Pretties, and the Gossip Girl series, while boys are prefer The Artemis Fowl, Cirque du Freak, Star Wars, Left Behind, and the Alex Rider Adventures series. Both girls and boys are crazy about Harry Potter.

For breezier fare, girls' first choice in magazines is *Seventeen*, while boys often pick up *Sports Illustrated*. Young males are also taken with gaming publications such as *GamePro* and *Nintendo Power*. In addition, both boys and girls put *TV Guide* on their top-five magazine lists.

Hanging at the Mall

When not playing sports, watching TV, surfing the Net, or reading, teens may be hanging out with friends at the nearest mall. More than 1,100 enclosed malls exist in the United States, and as many as 68 percent of teens spend at least some time in them in any given week. They go to see movies, shop, eat at the food court, connect with boyfriends or girlfriends, or just roam around with friends.

Although overall mall patronage has been declining for years, the number of teens in malls has greatly

The final Harry Potter book was released on July 21, 2007. It sold 8.3 million copies in the United States in the first 24 hours.

Teens are drawn to stores like Hot Topic because they follow popular trends.

increased. Girls are particularly avid mallgoers, in part because they love to shop. Young women under age 20 frequent specialty shops but tend to avoid larger department stores, which they associate with their mothers' shopping habits.

Mall management recognizes the importance of teens to sales. However, some adults feel the throngs of teens lead to obnoxious behavior. As a result, some malls have placed restrictions on teen shoppers. For instance, some mall policies require teens to be accompanied by adults after 6 P.M. on Fridays and Saturdays, if not every night.

Packed & Ready to Go

At some point, most teens journey farther away than the local mall for a trip. More than half of all teens help their parents choose family vacation destinations. Lodging facilities connected to theme parks (such as Disney World), amusement parks, and water parks have obvious teen appeal.

Orlando, Florida, the country's top tourist destination, is alive with theme and amusement park options. Teens (and parents, too) scream their way through Space Mountain and the Haunted Mansion at Walt Disney World's Magic Kingdom. At Disney-MGM Studios, they

Walt Disney World opened in 1971. About 46 million tourists visit annually.

plummet 13 stories in the Twilight Zone Tower of Terror and blast from zero to 60 miles (96 km) per hour in 2.8 seconds on the Rock 'n Roll Coaster. There's still more fun at Epcot Center and the Animal Kingdom, together with the area's non-Disney attractions.

Visiting friends and relatives is a popular family vacation, too. These jaunts are usually relatively short, often consisting of a three-day weekend. With both parents working, it is difficult to find extended periods in which both can get away from their jobs at the same time.

Camping trips top Americans' list of outdoor vacations. Catering to this demand, the U.S. National Park Service operates hundreds of campgrounds in parks that cover a total of 84 million acres (33.6 million hectares).

The most-visited national parks are the Great Smoky Mountains National Park in Tennessee, the Grand Canyon National Park in Arizona, Yosemite National Park in California, and Yellowstone National Park in Idaho, Montana, and Wyoming. From hiking toward the clouds to rafting down white waters, teens who visit these parks get their fill of fresh air. Indeed, nowhere else is "America the beautiful" more on display.

United States
Topographical map

N
W · E
S

0   150   300 mi.
0   150   300 km

Olympic National Park
Columbia River
Glacier National Park
Missouri River
CANADA
Great Lakes
CANADA
Acadia National Park
ROCKY
Cascade Range
Columbia Plateau
Theodore Roosevelt National Park
Isle Royale National Park
Yellowstone National Park
Crater Lake National Park
Grand Teton National Park
Devils Tower National Mon.
Hudson River
Coast Ranges
Sierra Nevada
Great Basin
Arches National Park
Badlands National Park
GREAT
Mississippi River
APPALACHIAN MOUNTAINS
Piedmont Plateau
ATLANTIC COASTAL PLAIN
Yosemite National Park
Zion National Park
Mesa Verde National Park
PLAINS
Ohio River
Mammoth Cave National Park
MOUNTAINS
Death Valley National Park
Grand Canyon National Park
Colorado Plateau
Arkansas River
Great Smoky Mts. National Park
Joshua Tree National Park
Colorado River
Red River
Mississippi River Basin
PACIFIC OCEAN
ATLANTIC OCEAN
ARCTIC OCEAN
RUSSIA
Gates of the Arctic Nat'l Park
CANADA
Big Bend National Park
Rio Grande
GULF COASTAL PLAIN
MEXICO
Orlando
Mt. McKinley
Denali National Park
Bering Sea
PACIFIC OCEAN
Gulf of Mexico
PACIFIC OCEAN
Everglades National Park
Hawai'i Volcanoes Nat'l Park

81

Looking Ahead

MANY AMERICAN TEENS HAVE COMFORTABLE HOMES, SOLID EDUCATIONS, AND NUMEROUS JOB OPPORTUNITIES. They attend middle schools, high schools, colleges, and universities, a majority of which offer well-rounded educations. They also have ample opportunities for part-time and sometimes full-time jobs that introduce them to the world of work. They enjoy rich holiday and religious traditions and celebrations, and have an enormous number of sports and other leisure activities to choose from. In short, society grants them untold choices; indeed, growing up in the United States is often a daily exercise in making choices.

These choices provide American teens with many life opportunities that millions of young people in poorer countries lack. The average U.S. teen has the freedom to open his or her mind to almost unlimited amounts of knowledge. That person can also aim to enter almost any profession or way of life. Compared with teens in many other countries, American teens have more than an even chance of enjoying long, fulfilling, and happy lives.

At a Glance

Official name: United States of America

Capital: Washington, D.C.

People

Population: 301,139,947

Population by age group:
0–14 years: 20.2%
15–64 years: 67.2%
65 years and over: 12.6%

Life expectancy at birth: 78 years

Common languages: English, Spanish, other Indo-European, various Asian

Religion:
Protestant: 52%
Roman Catholic: 24%
Mormon: 2%
Jewish: 1%
Muslim: 1%
Other: 10%
None: 10%

Legal ages:
Alcohol consumption: 21 years
Driver's license: Varies by state; 16 years average
Employment: 16 years, 14 with restrictions
Leave school: 16 years in 29 states; varies in others
Marriage: 18 without parental consent in all but two states: Nebraska, 19; Mississippi, 17 for males, 15 for females
Military service: 18; 17 years with parental consent
Voting: 18 years

Government

Type of government: Federal republic

Chief of state: President, elected for four-year terms by an electoral college, representatives who are elected directly from each state

Head of government: President

Lawmaking body: Congress consists of the Senate (100 seats), and the House of Representatives (435 seats), elected by popular vote

Administrative divisions: Fifty states and one district

Independence: July 4, 1776 (from Great Britain)

National symbols: Bald eagle, American flag, Great Seal of the United States

Geography

Total Area: 3,794,150 square miles (9,826,630 square kilometers)

Climate: Mostly temperate, but tropical in Hawaii and Florida, arctic in Alaska, semi-arid in the Great Plains west of the Mississippi River, arid in the Great Basin of the Southwest

Highest point: Mount McKinley, 20,320 feet (6,194 meters)

Lowest point: Death Valley, 282 feet (86 meters) below sea level

Major rivers: Arkansas, Colorado, Columbia, Hudson, Mississippi, Missouri, Ohio, Red, Rio Grande

Major landforms: Appalachian Mountains, Cascade Mountains, Rocky Mountains, Sierra Nevada Mountains, Eastern Coastal Plain, Great Plains, Columbia Plateau, Colorado Plateau, Piedmont Plateau, Great Basin

Economy

Currency: U.S. dollar (USD)

Population below poverty line: 12%

Major natural resources: Coal, copper, lead, phosphates, uranium, bauxite, gold, iron, mercury, nickel, potash, silver, tungsten, zinc, petroleum, natural gas, timber

Major agricultural products: Wheat, corn, fruits, potatoes, lettuce, tomatoes, mushrooms, onions, cotton, beef, pork, poultry, dairy products, fish, forest products

Major exports: Transistors, aircraft, motor vehicle parts, computers, telecommunications equipment, organic chemicals, automobiles, medicines, agricultural products

Major imports: Industrial supplies (including crude oil), automobiles, clothing, medicine, furniture, toys, computers, telecommunications equipment, vehicle parts, agricultural products

Historical Timeline

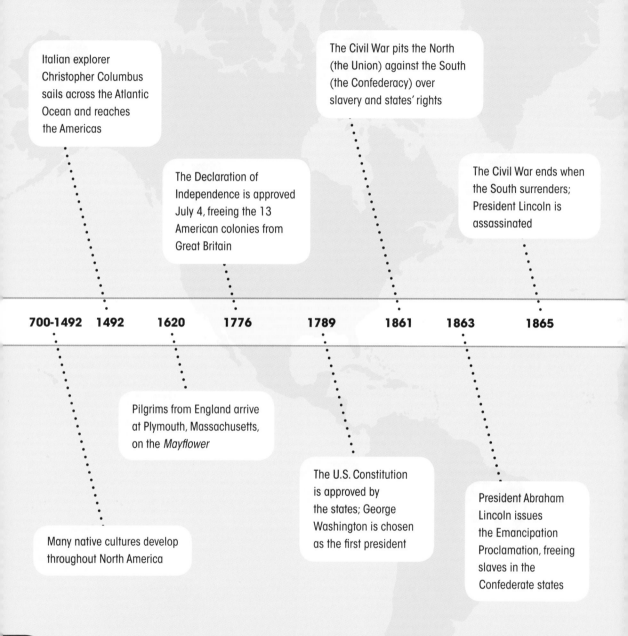

Italian explorer Christopher Columbus sails across the Atlantic Ocean and reaches the Americas

The Civil War pits the North (the Union) against the South (the Confederacy) over slavery and states' rights

The Declaration of Independence is approved July 4, freeing the 13 American colonies from Great Britain

The Civil War ends when the South surrenders; President Lincoln is assassinated

700-1492   1492   1620   1776   1789   1861   1863   1865

Pilgrims from England arrive at Plymouth, Massachusetts, on the *Mayflower*

The U.S. Constitution is approved by the states; George Washington is chosen as the first president

President Abraham Lincoln issues the Emancipation Proclamation, freeing slaves in the Confederate states

Many native cultures develop throughout North America

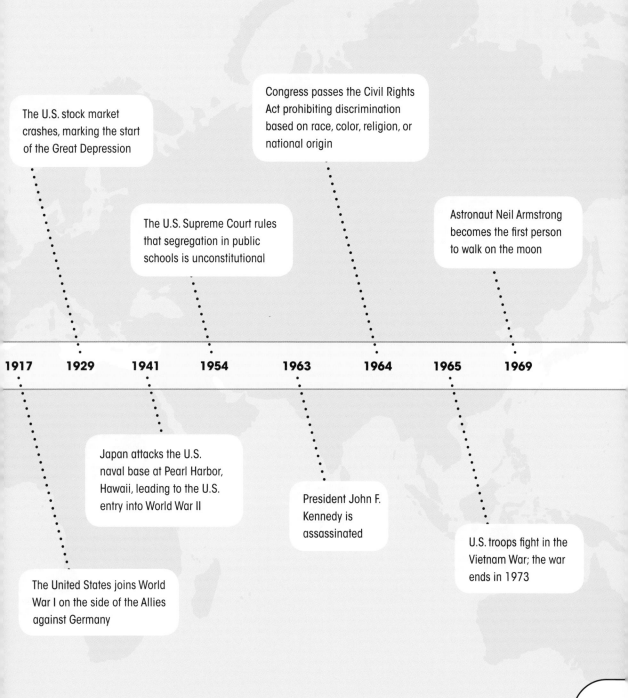

The U.S. stock market crashes, marking the start of the Great Depression

Congress passes the Civil Rights Act prohibiting discrimination based on race, color, religion, or national origin

The U.S. Supreme Court rules that segregation in public schools is unconstitutional

Astronaut Neil Armstrong becomes the first person to walk on the moon

1917   **1929**   **1941**   **1954**   **1963**   **1964**   **1965**   **1969**

Japan attacks the U.S. naval base at Pearl Harbor, Hawaii, leading to the U.S. entry into World War II

President John F. Kennedy is assassinated

U.S. troops fight in the Vietnam War; the war ends in 1973

The United States joins World War I on the side of the Allies against Germany

Historical Timeline

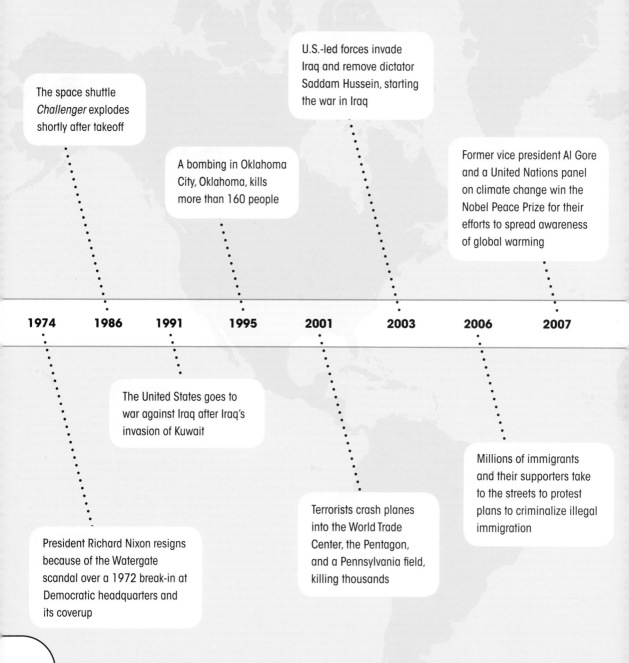

The space shuttle *Challenger* explodes shortly after takeoff

U.S.-led forces invade Iraq and remove dictator Saddam Hussein, starting the war in Iraq

A bombing in Oklahoma City, Oklahoma, kills more than 160 people

Former vice president Al Gore and a United Nations panel on climate change win the Nobel Peace Prize for their efforts to spread awareness of global warming

| 1974 | 1986 | 1991 | 1995 | 2001 | 2003 | 2006 | 2007 |

The United States goes to war against Iraq after Iraq's invasion of Kuwait

President Richard Nixon resigns because of the Watergate scandal over a 1972 break-in at Democratic headquarters and its coverup

Terrorists crash planes into the World Trade Center, the Pentagon, and a Pennsylvania field, killing thousands

Millions of immigrants and their supporters take to the streets to protest plans to criminalize illegal immigration

Glossary

baby boomers	those born in the United States between 1946 and 1965
commercial areas	portions of cities and towns that are devoted to business rather than private use
economic	related to the way a country produces, distributes, and uses its money, goods, natural resources, and services
extracurricular	referring to activities that occur outside a school's classes
immigrants	people who move from one country to live permanently in another
materialism	a strong attachment to material objects
poverty level	the level of income below which one cannot afford to buy the things necessary to live
retail	related to the sale of products or goods
service	providing a helpful activity rather than products or goods
subdivisions	areas of land that are divided into plots, each with a house built on it
suburbs	communities that are immediately outside of city limits; usually mostly residential areas
undergraduate	having to do with students who have not yet received a college degree
urbanized	characterized by dense populations and other qualities of city life
vocational-technical school	a school that prepares students to enter a career that requires skilled workers such as medical assistants, carpenters, or hair stylists

Additional Resources

FURTHER READING

Fiction and nonfiction titles to enhance your introduction to teens in the United States, past and present.

Brown, Don. *The Notorious Izzy Fink*. New Milford, Conn.: Roaring Brook Press, 2006.

Cofer, Judith Ortiz. *Call Me Maria*. New York: Orchard Books, 2003.

Curtis, Christopher Paul. *The Watsons Go to Birmingham—1963*. New York: Delacorte Press, 1995.

Shea, Pegi Deitz. *Tangled Threads: A Hmong Girl's Story*. New York: Clarion Books, 2003.

Son, John. *Finding My Hat*. New York: Orchard Books, 2003.

Waldman, Jackie. *Teens With the Courage to Give: Young People Who Triumphed Over Tragedy and Volunteered to Make a Difference*. Berkeley, Calf.: 2000.

ON THE WEB
For more information on this topic, use FactHound.
1. Go to www.facthound.com
2. Type in this book ID: 0756534089
3. Click on the Fetch It button.

Look for more Global Connections books.

Source Notes

Page 17, column 2, line 1: Akinyi R. "School Uniforms." *Teen Ink* June 2000. 2 Oct. 2007. www.teenink.com/Poetry/article.php?link=Past/2000/June/Opinion/SchoolUniforms.xml

Page 17, column 2, line 12: "Should Kids Be Required to Wear School Uniforms?" *Junior Scholastic* 4 Sept. 2006. The Free Library. 2 Oct. 2007. www.thefreelibrary.com/Should+kids+be+required+to+wear+school+uniforms%3F-a0150583914

Page 18, column 2, line 12: Chuck Offenburger. "School at Home." *eJournal USA: Society & Values* 10.1 (July 2005). 17 Oct. 2007. http://usinfo.state.gov/journals/itsv/0705/ijse/offenburger.htm

Page 34, sidebar, column 1, line 10: "Special Issues for Tweens and Teens." *Media Awareness Network*. 2007. 16 Oct. 2007. www.media-awareness.ca/english/parents/marketing/issues_teens_marketing.cfm?RenderForPrint=1

Page 42, sidebar, column 2, line 7: "In Their Own Words: Cross-Cultural Understanding." *eJournal USA: Society & Values* 10.1 (July 2005). 17 Oct. 2007. http://usinfo.state.gov/journals/itsv/0705/ijse/understanding.htm

Page 44, sidebar, line 6: "The United States Constitution." *The U.S. Constitution Online*. 31 July 2007. 22 Oct. 2007. www.usconstitution.net/const.html#Am1

Page 44, line 8: "In Their Own Words: Influence of Religion." *eJournal USA: Society & Values* 10.1 (July 2005). 17 Oct. 2007. http://usinfo.state.gov/journals/itsv/0705/ijse/religion.htm

Page 69, line 22: "In Their Own Words: Volunteering." *eJournal USA: Society & Values* 10.1 (July 2005). 17 Oct. 2007. http://usinfo.state.gov/journals/itsv/0705/ijse/volunteer.htm

Page 74, column 2, line 4: Tom Pryor. "Hip Hop." *National Geographic World Music*. 2007. 18 Oct. 2007. http://worldmusic.nationalgeographic.com/worldmusic/view/page.basic/genre/content.genre/hip_hop_730

Pages 84–85, At a Glance: United States. Central Intelligence Agency. *The World Factbook—United States*. 18 Oct. 2007. 23 Oct. 2007. https://www.cia.gov/library/publications/the-world-factbook/geos/us.html

Select Bibliography

Abma, J.C., G.M. Martinez, W.D. Mosher, and B.S. Dawson. Teenagers in the United States: Sexual Activity, Contraceptive Use, and Childbearing, 2002. National Center for Health Statistics 23 (24). 2004. 12 Nov. 2007. http://cdc.gov/nchs/data/series/sr_23/sr23_024.pdf

Austin, Joe. *Generations of Youth*. New York: New York University Press, 1998.

Berland, Marcela M. "A Promising Hispanic Market." *Hispanic Magazine.com*. April 2004. 5 May 2007. http://hispaniconline.com/magazine/2004/april/Forum/index.html

Burns, Kate, ed. *Examining Pop Culture: The American Teenager*. Farmington Hills, Mich.: Greenhaven Press, 2003.

Eisenberg, Paul, ed. *Fodor's USA 28th Edition*. Fodor's Travel Publications. New York: Random House, 2003.

Grier, Peter, and Sara B. Miller. "Incredible Shrinking US Family." *The Christian Science Monitor*. 2 Dec. 2004. 12 Nov. 2007. www.csmonitor.com/2004/1202/p01s01-ussc.html

Hersch, Patricia. *A Tribe Apart: A Journey Into the Heart of American Adolescence*. New York: Ballantine, 1999.

"In Their Own Words: Cross-Cultural Understanding." *eJournal USA: Society & Values* 10.1 (July 2005). 17 Oct. 2007. http://usinfo.state.gov/journals/itsv/0705/ijse/understanding.htm

"In Their Own Words: Influence of Religion." *eJournal USA: Society & Values* 10.1 (July 2005). 17 Oct. 2007. http://usinfo.state.gov/journals/itsv/0705/ijse/religion.htm

"In Their Own Words: Volunteering." *eJournal USA: Society & Values* 10.1 (July 2005). 17 Oct. 2007. http://usinfo.state.gov/journals/itsv/0705/ijse/volunteer.htm

Kantrowitz, Barbara, and Anne Underwood. "The Teen Drinking Dilemma." *Newsweek* 25 June 2007, pp. 36–37.

Millar, Heather. "The Hidden Epidemic of Very Young Alcoholics." *Good Housekeeping* May 2007, pp. 177–181, 242–244.

Offenburger, Chuck. "School at Home." *eJournal USA: Society & Values* 10.1 (July 2005). 17 Oct. 2007. http://usinfo.state.gov/journals/itsv/0705/ijse/offenburger.htm

Palladino, Grace. *Teenagers: An American History.* New York: BasicBooks, 1996.

Pryor, Tom. "Hip Hop." *National Geographic World Music.* 2007. 18 Oct. 2007. http://worldmusic.nationalgeographic.com/worldmusic/view/page.basic/genre/content.genre/hip_hop_730

Quart, Alissa. *Branded: The Buying and Selling of Teenagers.* Cambridge, Mass.: Perseus Pub., 2003.

R., Akinyi. "School Uniforms." *Teen Ink* June 2000. 2 Oct. 2007. www.teenink.com/Poetry/article.php?link=Past/2000/June/Opinion/SchoolUniforms.xml

"Should Kids Be Required to Wear School Uniforms?" *Junior Scholastic* 4 Sept. 2006. The Free Library. 2 Oct. 2007. www.thefreelibrary.com/Should+kids+be+required+to+wear+school+uniforms%3F-a0150583914

"Special Issues for Tweens and Teens." *Media Awareness Network.* 2007. 16 Oct. 2007. www.media-awareness.ca/english/parents/marketing/issues_teens_marketing.cfm?RenderForPrint=1

Summerill, Lynette. "The Chore of Chores." *ASU Research.* (Fall 2001). 12 Nov. 2007. www.asu.edu/research/researchmagazine/2001Fall/Fall01p10-11.pdf

"Teaching Appreciation Diminishes the Impact of Materialism." *HarrisInteractive.* 8 Jan. 2007. 5 Nov. 2007. www.harrisinteractive.com/news/allnewsbydate.asp?NewsID=1141

"The United States Constitution." *The U.S. Constitution Online.* 31 July 2007. 22 Oct. 2007. www.usconstitution.net/const.html#Am1

United States. Census Bureau. Educational Attainment in the United States: 2006. 9 Nov. 2007. www.census.gov/population/www/socdemo/education/cps2006.html

United States. Census Bureau. State and Country Quickfacts. 31 Aug. 2007. 9 Nov. 2007. http://quickfacts.census.gov/qfd/states/00000.html

United States. Central Intelligence Agency. *The World Factbook—United States.* 18 Oct. 2007. 23 Oct. 2007. https://www.cia.gov/library/publications/the-world-factbook/geos/us.html

United States. Department of Education. National Center for Education Statistics. *The Condition of Education.* Washington, D.C., 2003–2007.

United States. Department of Labor: Bureau of Labor Statistics. "Tomorrow's Jobs." 20 Dec. 2005. 12 Nov. 2007. www.bls.gov/oco/oco2003.htm

United States. Social Security Administration. "Popular Baby Names by Decade." 6 March 2007. 8 Nov. 2007. www.ssa.gov/OACT/babynames/decades/names2000s.html

Index

About the Author
Kitty Shea

Kitty Shea has authored books for young readers, served as editor of home and travel magazines, edited cookbooks, and published hundreds of articles and essays. Kitty Shea has also taught in the journalism department of her alma mater, the University of St. Thomas in St. Paul, Minnesota.

About the Content Adviser
Sasha Vliet,
Ph.D. candidate

Sasha Vliet is part of the American Studies department at the University of Texas, where she has taught courses on youth culture. A former high school teacher, her research interests are youth, youth culture, education, public schooling, and youth expression.